Where is MY AMERICA

T.Germann

DEDICATION

This book is dedicated to the HOPE that it is not too late to save our country from the politicians that have destroyed it. Many thanks to the service people who have served, fought and given all in defense and service to this great country. Please visit www.USA.gov and look up your elected officials and if you agree with what is written in this book, send a copy to them and to candidates running for office. They need to know we truly have had enough.

CONTENTS

Acknowledgments i

1 Politicians 1

2 Social Security 14

3 Insurance 16

4 Stop The Madness 18

ACKNOWLEDGMENTS

It seems we are all consumed with work, television, social networking or other distractions to care or notice what is happening in our country. I'm no PhD Political Science guru and have no special skills of insight into anything. What I do have is a case of the red ass and will use this as an avenue to delve into a few things. If a politician wants my two cents, run on a platform of America First. Spend money on OUR infrastructure first, feed OUR hungry and clothe OUR poor before sending a single taxpayer dollar abroad. This isn't rocket science. I increasingly feel alienated in the very country I love and one day I looked around and asked myself, where is MY America? Have you seen YOURS lately? If not, what are YOU doing about it?

God Bless the American People

1 POLITICIANS

Where to start on the business of holding a public office. Yes, I said BUSINESS, because to the majority of office holders, it is a business. Once elected they are dazzled with a welcoming package. The higher the office, the greater the perks. I won't go off into a rant on what these perks are, but let's just agree that they receive access to special perks that the public is unaware of and will never receive themselves. Special banking privileges, control over voting oneself a raise, special retirement and insurance. Even the laws of the land are different in many respects for them as they carefully exempted themselves from the unsavory laws they passed that you and I are forced to accept. The thought of it makes my blood boil. How dare they? Just who do they think they are and why is no one doing anything about it? There are many who are A LOT smarter than I on the subject and inside details of politics but I am a competent, educated and thinking person that isn't blind to the obvious. A person could write volumes on the many, many ways in which the system could be tweaked, but I am going to throw a few things out there. We, the citizens of the United States need to demand some accountability and demand some action from our law makers. We employ them and provide the funds for them to spend, and then watch in silence as WE are ripped off. The biggest thing I think we can do which would fundamentally change politics as they have become, is to end politics as a career. I'm talking about term limits for ALL positions. Ride with me down this road for a while. The men and women get elected and may be full of energy and ideals when first elected but as they are indoctrinated into the perks, power and privilege of politics, they become swayed and romanced by big business, campaign dollars and tickets to special events which they soon come to expect, and do so unashamedly. We are fools to continue to allow people, no matter how good intentioned at one time, to become career politicians. The temptation to see themselves as above the general population is too great. The separation between them and the people only grows over time and so many are out of touch and unaware of it. Others are quite aware, but are so entrenched in the world they have grown accustomed to, a world of perks, power and privilege, that they will lie, scheme and deceive openly to hold on to office. We need to end this. We need to pull our lawmakers from our ranks, send them to vote for the good of all and then accept them back into our ranks where they are subject to the same laws they passed. It's a novel idea, but why should they be exempt from the same laws, the same insurance, the same retirement, the same banks, loans that WE ALL get? Don't leave them in office long enough to become corrupt and entrenched. To begin to feel they are separate from the people and entitled to a lifetime of care, salary, insurance or other perks. Wouldn't it make more sense to set a limit for how long they can serve? Sure we need some experienced politicians that have been around long enough to understand how to get things done and to understand complex issues, but after two or maybe three terms, its times for them to return back to being one of us; a citizen. How can we expect people in office who are not subject to our insurance, retirement and laws to understand our perspectives on these things and act in our best interest? Term limits are a must. We should also remove these perks they receive. Take down the wall that separates them from us. Some will argue that these special perks are to give them compensation that will keep them from being tempted. Hogwash! They set these perks up for themselves. Until they are subject to each and every law that we citizens are subject to, get the same retirement we citizens get, pay the same in taxes, use the same banks and know with certainty that they will be returning to face the circumstances they built while in office, we will not see change. With term limitations, they won't have such long periods to hide their connections to special interest or learn to hide affiliations. They would be more likely to get caught if acting inappropriately with special interest groups because of the shorter terms. Who really notices if a Senator meets 70 times with a particular group over the course of 30 or 40 years? But it would quickly raise interest and notice if the same were to occur in a short period of time. While on this point of this topic, why in the hell do we allow political action committees to carry on mostly unchecked. They sway lawmakers hugely as compared to you or me, so wouldn't we want to know what they are pushing to our lawmakers, limit their campaign contributions GREATLY. How many go around limitations through fake companies, promise jobs or other financial benefits in hopes of buying influence. We as citizens, do NOT have the weight of ALL things on our shoulders to repair. Yes, the infrastructure needs repair, the poor need tending, the healthcare system needs re-working, our debt is out of control and our government spending is beyond comprehension. But if we fix our political problem, in short order we will begin to see solutions to problems. We would have lawmakers who go in knowing they will be returning to the mess that exists and have to work on solutions instead of entrenching themselves in the world of separated privilege. I am sickened by the government we have had for the past 20 years. Especially the new ultra-liberal extremist which have pulled an constitutional coup using presidential orders to pass laws which the people did not want, that violated our constitution and forced the productive citizens to bear the burdens for many who we feel do not deserve our tax dollars. The few who would speak out are called uncaring racists or hateful and selfish when so many are in need. But I see it differently. I see many people who won't put forth the effort to better themselves and desire special treatment. I see poor illegal immigrants grasping at our welfare, healthcare and over-burdening our schools. Does saying these things make me a racist or uncaring? Am I turning my back on my fellow man? Should the government tell me who gets MY money? Who I will care for? It's MY business not theirs. You can't regulate charity or spirit of giving. My view is that those who are in this country illegally, are just that, illegal. Lawbreakers. Just as any other lawbreaker, they should be held accountable for violating our laws, face penalties, deported and as a new punishment for violating our borders, those that are caught should lose the ability to come legally. To me, by demonstrating a propensity and willingness to violate our laws, they have shown their disregard for us, our country and the rule of law and in by doing so, give up the ability to come LEGALLY. Let's welcome the non-lawbreakers who follow our laws and legally come to our country. The ones who are illegal should under no circumstances receive, aid, benefits, welfare or citizenship via anchor babies they birthed while here illegally. That's MY tax money that is getting spent on those who are not entitled to it. How much money would this put back into our welfare, food stamp, medical and school systems? Would it also ease crime? What?! Another racist statement? No.

Doesn't it reason that those who demonstrate willingness to break out laws will continue to do so? I can hear the irrational and illogical wanting to argue and bring up exceptions to this, but don't bother. I won't entertain those irrelevant arguments any longer. I'm sick of hearing exceptions given to justify a law or response that affects the whole nation. My ancestors came here from another country. They came legally and then assimilated. They learned the language, to speak and write the language of this country and became American. They served our military and flew the American flag. Yes, they had cultural pride in the country of origin, but first and foremost, they were proud to be Americans. They didn't fly the flag of the country they came from on their homes, businesses and cars, demand taxpayers hire interpreters and print documents in their former native language. That would be disrespectful and an unfair burden to expect the American people to spend their money to accommodate them and actually assist in helping them NOT assimilate. I also feel women shouldn't be on the front lines in combat situations. Sure there are exceptions to that and even good exceptions, but there are more reasons and logic supporting my take on it. Do I want to convince you of this? No. It's my opinion. Was it a sexist statement? Maybe. Depends on if my opinion was based on facts and sound reasoning or if it's said because I feel women aren't up to the task. There will be those who will call you a racist and sexist with no facts, so why worry. I had a woman who was upset because I support a person's constitutional right to own a firearm call me names and then say what else can you expect from someone from the South. This is the mentality and reasoning skills that are guiding our future and it scares the hell out of me. The few are controlling the many and every little twist or nuance of thought or lifestyle now thinks it is entitled to acceptance and funding. Homosexual lifestyles are another thing that has recently reached a point where I feel it has gone too far. To everything, every behavior, there must be a line drawn someplace. Some will say that's not true; why can't everyone "do their own thing". So should there really be no lines? Should exhibitionists be allowed to do "their" thing at work, church, public restaurants? Do you want to sit on chairs or bike seats at the bike rental place while on vacation that nudists used before you while doing "their thing"? The list could continue but surely the point can be seen that lines must be drawn somewhere. If you want to be homosexual or are homosexual, by all means carry on. But do not call me a hater when I refuse to watch TV shows or shop at businesses where they present homosexual story lines or present commercials depicting homosexual couples on primetime TV as if it's normal. I don't want my kids raised thinking it is and I don't want them exposed to it. Most people in the gay community know what I am talking about as many of them too are embarrassed by the ones that flaunt the lifestyle and take pride in the discomfort they can cause others in the name of promoting "their thing". I'm also sorry for them that marriage was defined as between a man and a woman long ago and that doesn't fall into that lifestyle. I think you should be able to visit a lawyer, draw up whatever contract between you and your relationship partner that protects you both, allows you to share property, insurance, retirement, etc. Pursue what makes you happy but you don't get to do it at the expense of everyone else around you who don't share "your thing". Call your union something else other than marriage. That one is already in use and has been for a long, long time. It's like a small group deciding that the color blue will continue to mean blue to most folks but everyone must also accept that to your group, it's also green. Give it a rest. The same goes for ownership of firearms. A small group of vocal folks want to tell the millions of lawful owners of firearms what they can and can't own in some misguided and illogical idea that it will affect crime rates. As if criminals care what the laws are. Making drugs illegal has stopped drug use too right?! The politicians that give these ideas weight and decide to propose legislation geared to appease such a small group by imposing it on the masses need to be removed from representing the masses. Term limits my friend. It will give the population greater control over the direction we as a country move.

My intent isn't to inflame people, the small groups or those who think differently. You're welcome to your thoughts, but stop trying to force them on me. We all draw "the line" somewhere; this is where I've drawn mine.

Politicians and our military. Leave the running of our military to the Generals. By creating these rules of engagement that are so different to the situations our young people are facing, you are causing deaths. Deaths! Of our young people who serve and protect! Do you get that? They should be well armed, well trained, well protected and free to act as needed to protect themselves. Stop sending them to regions where we have no business. War is a last resort. But once we feel we must commit to war, do not send a few troops, and few bombs. Rain down the thunder and come to a fast, decisive conclusion with minimal loss of life for OUR troops. In the Middle East we watched as snipers would fire on our soldiers and then retreat into a church because they knew our rules would not allow us to strike the church. It became a sanctuary for them. The enemy would fire weapons at our troops, run behind something, then lay down weapons and simply walk away, unable to be fired upon because they stopped their threat. Who wrote these rules? If they are allowed to take sanctuary in a church after firing at our troops, the country should be aware we WILL flatten that structure. It is war, and we will not risk our soldiers lightly. There is no sanctuary if you fire on our troops. Any why do the politicians turn the country back over after the war is won? Perhaps a countries people would reconsider their actions towards others if they knew they were risking everything by attacking others. That if they wake the sleeping giant by killing its innocents, we WILL come, we WILL be many, we WILL NOT come lightly and we when the job is done, we will NOT be returning your country to you. If we spill American blood on foreign soil, we should plant a flag. That government should cease to exist and its treasury looted to recoup the cost of the war. I read the stories of military officers transferring themselves or networking to have themselves transferred into a safe zone within a combat area just so they could get a promotion, a medal or combat patch and pay even they were not in much danger and were NOT IN COMBAT. This would have been a big deal and all over the news just a couple of decades ago. Disgusting. For the troops that were actually in combat? It is my opinion that they are heroes. They should NEVER pay Federal income taxes again. They paid their debt to this country. I can hear the politicians cringing because its tax dollars they won't get to spend and we are SO in debt. How do you think we got there morons? You spent us there. It's not like you didn't have enough. We are taxed heavily and you get enough from us. You get too much! You spend it on pork barrel projects, unnecessary contracts that are over-priced as rewards to those who supported your latest campaign. You should be arrested for treason and betrayal of the American people. Our country needs a time of isolationism to a large extent. A period where the world will have to manage itself because we aren't sending

funds to prop up other governments, feed the hungry on
the other side of the world, or supporting political turmoil
in another country. Instead, we need that money here.
America First. Brings jobs home. Politicians would have
you believe it's the high wages of American workers that
drive companies overseas. That's not necessarily true.
It's the red tape; the government intrusion into business
and requirements placed on companies that bleed them of
both profits and efficiency. It's a lot to comply with
mountains of ridiculous layers of red tape. I'm not
guessing at this folks. I own a small business. I bought
my building. Paid taxes, then continue paying property
taxes. Then a fee to occupy the building, inspection fees,
fees to upgrade the building to bring it to the new code
then more inspection fees, then fees for the privilege of
conducting business within the city, fees for conducting
business within the county, fees for conducting business
within the state, state permit fees, federal permit fees, all
renewable and must be paid again within a year or two,
then county taxes on the equipment I place in the
building in order to conduct business (due yearly) and
don't forget that I paid sales tax when I purchased that
equipment in the first place, then there is state franchise
tax which is based on the income the business makes
providing it turns any profit, then for every employee we
provide a job to, we must not only withhold taxes from
their check and make regular deposits to the government
of that withheld money, but as the employer we must also
match much of that withheld money, and then finally pay

federal income tax if we have anything left to call profit but we don't know that till we hire a tax professional who has dedicated their education and profession to making sense of the overly complex taxation system. If the government wanted to create jobs and spark prosperity again among its people it could simply get its hands out of the pocket of the small businesses and remove the barriers that overly complicate the average person from owning a small business. Why do they drag their feet in making a fair tax system instead of cooking the numbers for different income brackets so they can try to maximize their take? A flat percentage which is applied to everyone regardless of their bracket is FAIR and JUST, what hard to understand about that. It would also uncomplicated our tax determination and save people money who are so confused of the current system that they feel they must pay others to do it for them. Where are the politicians in finding real solutions? Government aid (welfare) needs limits. Time limits on how long it can be received. Sure some have true debilitating circumstances where they will need a lifetime of assistance. But too fat to work is usually not an easily accepted condition that warrants a lifetime of our money. I don't want to pay for that. People who make poor personal choices and end up in dire circumstances with no income or education and job skills are facing a tragedy. Give them a hand up not hand out. Supply them with a job or job training, community college AND welfare for a limited period of time. They get the shot they never had, housing, food, and training.

Then it ends. If they choose to not avail themselves to the assistance, I don't want to support them, their children and so on for the rest of their lives. Give them an honest chance. If they blow it, spend MY money elsewhere. People are responsible for themselves. Leave the welfare for those with real disabilities, injuries and lifelong need.

2 SOCIAL SECURITY

A good idea gone wrong is what social security is. How long will we let OUR money be stolen? Why do I say stolen? We pay into it our entire working lives. If we own businesses, we not only pay into it for ourselves but our businesses match the payments our employees make. Does it go into an account for our safe keeping? No, it's spent immediately. The total of the money even at a simple interest rate would sustain us well till the end of our lives. It was intended to provide income for us in our old age and for what remains of our family. But how many die before everything we paid in gets paid out? How many die before even receiving a penny of what they pay in? Why is that money not returned to the rightful survivors? Not only are we paying a large percentage of our wages in income taxes but these "remains" of our payments to social security are kept as well. Add the percentages together along with every other tax we pay, sales, property, school etc and it's no wonder Americans are struggling. This money is ours! We earned it by WORKING and trusted it to be there when we are old. But it gets kept and spent if we die.

Our surviving spouse gets left to choose between their own social security or that of their departed spouse. That money was theirs and should be given back to them. It's not a gift, it's not a "program", it belongs to them that earned it. Why does our government need SO much money? So the politicians can grant lopsided overstuffed contracts to their supporters, so we can send billions in aid to other countries or finance other things that do not benefit the American people. And still the money is not enough. We must borrow many billions from others to continue. Print money at our mints that is unweighted and unsupported by our economy. For what purpose? When will the financial stupidity end? Is it too late to regain our once proud standing in the world? Only when the people stop being passive and pay attention to the votes our lawmakers cast, place limits and controls will the people control it rather than it control them. This chapter takes so little room to cover, it's simple to understand. This money is our money and we pay hundreds every single week for the length of our work lives. It is ours, and we want it back from our government. Talk about how short the program is going to be and when it will run out of money and how we must work longer to have the honor of getting our money back so we can retire and rest. I don't want socialism, I want my money and for them to butt out of controlling the time I retire and the money I worked for.

3 INSURANCE

The government passed laws requiring automobile insurance. Its common place now, but anytime we are REQUIRED by law to PAY, it's a tax. In this case its money to go to private insurance companies. A good idea to have insurance, but alas, only if the scope in which its being viewed is narrow. How much are you spending on insurance a month? Can you afford it? Or are you a "criminal" driving without insurance because you must pay rent or buy food? How long till your "caught" and face a heavy fine? If so you will likely pay a higher premium once you try to comply with the law. But it's all for the good right? In case you need it. I've had vehicle insurance since licensed to the tune of tens of thousands of dollars. There are over 200 million licensed drivers in this country. Working the math you quickly see where insurance on one's car is feasible and prudent for the people who can afford it. But for the poor, it's a drain on their already tight budgets, forcing many to skirt the laws and become "criminals" to pay huge sums of money to private companies under the direct threat of law to be enforced by your government. I'm not feeling warm and fuzzy. What about medical insurance? Now we are talking some REAL dollars. IF you're lucky enough to have medical insurance, how much is it? $300 a month to $500 a month if I had to guess. Again, for those that can afford it, it's wonderful. So many do not. Why is it so expensive? Why is an aspirin in the hospital cost $10? A piece of tape for an IV a patient is charged nothing at some places, at others, several dollars. Who cares, insurance is paying it right? Who cares if a doctor charges $45,000 for an hour long surgery? After all, the cost of the room, supplies, nurses, anesthesia all have to be paid for right? Do you know how much doctors pay for malpractice INSURANCE? Yep, insurance again. Remove some red tape, allow patients to sign waivers that protect doctors from all but true bad practice, or change the laws to prevent frivolous suits. Stop the AMA from protecting bad doctors. Do something that makes sense for a change and benefits the people. Doctors wont cease being just because they don't have a European Super Car and mansion. Many would be content making a nice salary and helping people if the whole mess could be unraveled a bit and they be left to practice medicine.

4 STOP THE MADNESS

Instead of using common sense, the silent distracted
majority sit and watch the small groups who are vocal
and active steer new directions of madness. Our
Constitution is ignored or in cases of national security as
they call it, suspended. You can be stopped, searched,
arrested, detained, watched, or killed if you are called the
right thing. No process of law, no trial, no open
production of evidence. Simple Constitutional violations
that's all. It's fine with all of you right? It's not with me.
Instead of simply dealing with the existing problems
which are great, we create new unchartered slippery
slopes to slide down. Strengths given to agencies that
they should never have. Our lawmakers MUST act on the
behalf of the people. We must stop being too busy and
too distracted to let our voices be heard. We need new
leaders who will use common sense to stop this decline.
Where is my America? Where is OUR America? It's fine
if you disagree with me. But if you agree, please take

another step. Tell your representatives and senators that you want this debt stopped. Tell them you want your social security back, you want a reduction in red tape for small businesses. Take 10 minutes of your social networking time and give them a call, tell them you've had enough and you want YOUR America back. If you want our constitution supported, then tell them so. Let them know that you oppose billions going to aid other countries when we need help here at home and our debt erased. Consider running for office and introduce bills to limit terms and end the special privileges and exemptions of our law makers. Push back. There's a radio host in Houston, Texas by the name of Michael Berry. I recognize him as a true American. He isn't playing the politically correct game. He uses common sense and speaks things as he sees them. For that, I'm sure he gets crazy calls, threats and is probably told to be more agreeable. But that's my point, we must all start to stand up, and demand something different that makes sense to us. Sure we all see things a little differently, but if we continue to allow these few hundred lawmakers to determine the fate of our country and the millions of people continue to be fleeced and misled, we truly are a defeated nation and I refuse to believe that. The Republicans and the Democrats have the American people confused and they use this to keep THEM in power instead of the American people.

God Bless you and God Bless America.